An Introduction

WILLIAM BARNES

• THE DORSET POET •

1801-1886

DOUGLAS ASHDOWN

DORSET BOOKS

First published in Great Britain in 1996 by Dorset Books

Reprinted 1999

British Library Cataloguing-in-Publication Data
A CIP Catalogue Record for this book is available from the British Library

ISBN 1 871164 25 7

DORSET BOOKS
Official Publisher to Dorset County Council

Halsgrove House
Lower Moor Way
Tiverton, EX16 6SS

Telephone: 01884 243242
Facsimile: 01884 243325

Front cover: The first known photograph of Rev. William Barnes, taken in 1852. (Courtesy Dorset County Museum).
Back Cover: Solicitor Thomas Henry Dashwood's house, Sturminster Newton. It was here that William Barnes was first employed as a clerk in 1814. (Author).

Printed and bound in Great Britain by
Culm Print, Tiverton

Contents

To Brenda

Acknowledgements

This book would not have been published without the help of Carleton Earl, Dorset County Librarian.

'Sun-prints' and engravings have been provided by kind permission of the Dorset County Library and the Dorset County Museum; my 'pen-hand' has been my good neighbour Mrs Marion Cox, a journalist, who has given me considerable assistance.

I am indebted to many members of the William Barnes Society for their friendship and support, particularly Trevor Hearl, Fred Langford, Mrs Jill Bryant, Dr Alan Chedzoy and Dr Charlotte Lindgren of Boston, USA.

In the course of my research the frontline staff of the Dorset County Library, Dorchester and the County Record Office have become my friends. To Nick Lawrence, Shirley, Val and Julie of the Dorset County Library reference section and to Helen, Peter and particularly Raymond at the County Record Office: thank you.

Hugh Jacques, Dorset County Archivist; Richard de Peyer, Curator, Dorset County Museum, and Judith Stinton; Mrs Madge Wheat and her staff of the Family History Centre, IGI, Mount Road, Parkstone; and all those many unnamed young archivists and librarians throughout the country who have replied to my enquiries, have all been unfailingly helpful.

I must record my thanks to Trevor Hearl, Lloyd Thomas, Cassell & Co., J. Stevens Cox and the Dovecote Press, for illustrations and photographs.

Above all my wife Brenda who has been a model of understanding and everlasting patience.

Dorchester, Dorset.
1996

A List of Dates

1801 Born 22 February at Rush-Hay, Bagber, Sturminster Newton, the fifth child of John and Grace Barnes. Baptised 29 March 1801 at Sturminster Newton Parish Church. John Barnes was a 'labourer in husbandry', kept a 'farmling' although he would have grazed his limited stock of farm animals on the common land.

William Barnes was educated at the Sturminster Newton Endowed Parish School 1810 to 1814. He was a bright pupil, interested in all subjects. His 'mate' was his cousin Charlie Roberts, son of Charles and Ann Roberts who lived nearby at Pentridge Farm.

1814 Employed as a clerk in the office of Thomas Dashwood, Solicitor, Sturminster Newton.

1816 21 January his mother dies. Thomas Dashwood dies. He becomes unemployed. Moves to Dorchester.

1818 Employed as an engrossing clerk in the office of Thomas Coombs, Solicitor, 5 South Street, Dorchester. Studies engraving, languages and music in his free time.

1819 Meets Julia Miles, daughter of Excise Officer James Miles and his wife Isabella Miles. The Miles, with their eight sons and two daughters had been living in South Street from about 1812.

1820 *Poetical Pieces*; printed by G.Clark, Dorchester.

1822 *Orra: A Lapland Tale*; printed by J. Criswick, Dorchester.

1823 Moved to Mere, Wiltshire to open his own school in the loft of the Market House.

1827 Rented Chantry House, Mere, early June. Married Julia Miles 9 July at Nailsea, nr Bristol. Immediately opens a mixed day and boarding school.

1828 Daughter Laura Liebe born.

1832 Daughter Julia Eliza born.

1834 His first Dorset dialect poem published in the *Dorset County Chronicle*, 2 February. Son Julius born.

1835 Returned to Dorchester. Opened a day and boarding school in a 'straight-up penthouse' in Durngate Street.

1837 School overcrowded. Sickness throughout the Durngate Street property. Son Julius dies and is discreetly buried. A barren period for Barnes. Lucy Emily born 21 January.

1838 22 January opens school at Norman's House, 17 South Street. Accepted, as a 'Ten year man', on the books of St John's College, Cambridge to study for Bachelor of Divinity Degree. Daughter Isabel born.

1840 Son William Miles born.

1841 His friend Edward Fuller dies and leaves him £100.

1843 Son Egbert born.

1844 *Poems in the Dorset Dialect* (first collection) published. Visits London as guest of the Hon. Caroline Norton.

1845 A prosperous time. Buys land at Sturminster Newton. Lends money on mortgage. Co-founder of Dorset County Museum. Railways come to Dorchester. Barnes and others prevent railway companies from destroying Poundbury and Maumbury Rings, Roman sites.

1846 *Poems of Rural Life in National English* published. Failed to secure mastership of the Dorchester Free Grammar School [Hardye's School].

1847 Ordained Curate of Whitcombe, near Dorchester 28 February with a stipend of £13 per year. Attends St John's College, Cambridge. Buys and moves to 40 South Street (Hawkin's House) for £700 and builds additional classrooms.

1849 *Se Gefylsta: An Anglo-Saxon Delectus. Humilis Domus: Some Thoughts on the Abodes, Life and Social Conditions of the Poor, Especially in Dorsetshire.* Cholera epidemic in the Fordington area of Dorchester.

1850 Awarded Bachelor of Divinity Degree by St John's College, Cambridge. *Hwomely Rhymes;* a second collection of Dorset poems published.

1851 Visits the Great Exhibition in London with his wife and two daughters.

1852 His wife, his 'beloved Julia' dies from cancer of the breast, 21 June. School begins to decline. Laura, the eldest daughter, aged twenty-three years, takes charge of the family as well as the school boarding. Laura never married; she looked after her father for the rest of his life.

1853 Begins and continues for many years to give poetry readings and lectures throughout Wessex.

1854 *A Philological Grammar ... formed from a comparison of more than sixty languages.*

1858 *Notes on Ancient Britain.*

1859 School in real decline. His children begin to leave home. Julia travels to Germany and Florence for voice training. Lucy begins to write novelettes. Son Willie enters St John's College, Cambridge. Egbert starts engineering apprenticeship at the Railway Works, Swindon. *Views of Labour and Gold* published. A second collection of Dorset dialect poems.

1860 Youngest daughter Isabel marries Rev. J. Shaw, 21 June. They move to Cumbria.

1861 Shaw dies 14 April leaving a great deal of money and property to Isabel. Isabel returns to family home in Dorchester. Barnes is given a Civil List literary pension of £70 a year awarded by Queen Victoria.

1862 30 January Barnes offered the living at Winterborne Came by his former pupil Capt. Dawson Damer. The offer is accepted. His school closes 20 June. *'TIW' or a View of the roots and stems of the English as a Teutonic tongue.*

1863 Julia marries Charles Dunn. They live permanently in Florence. *A Grammar and Glossary of the Dorset Dialect.* Third collection of *Poems in the Dorset Dialect.*

1865 Willie receives his BA degree from St John's College, Cambridge. Is ordained Deacon and then Priest at Salisbury Cathedral. Throughout this decade Barnes continues to write papers for *Macmillan's Magazine, The Reader, Frazer's Magazine,* etc.

1866 Egbert marries Jane Creasy from Swindon on 25 June. Willie inducted to the living at Winterborne Monkton.

1867 Willie marries Emily le Cocq from the Channel Islands on 20 June.

1868 Lucy Emily visits Florence. She is escorted through France and Italy by Thomas Baxter. They marry almost immediately and live permanently in Florence. *Poems of Rural Life in Common English.*

1869 *Early England and the Saxon-English.*

1872 First collected edition of *Poems in the Dorset Dialect.*

1873 Egbert dies 27 September.

1882 The rich widow Isabel Shaw marries Thomas Dent Gardener, a wealthy London solicitor. Despite his age Barnes continues to attend to the needs of his parish.

1885 Barnes is ill but still writing. Dictates his last poem *The Geate a-Vallen to'.* Throughout the twenty-four years he lived at Came Rectory he is visited by eminent men of letters, Edmund Gosse, Coventry Patmore, Francis Palgrave, Lord Tennyson and his young neighbour Thomas Hardy.

1886 Died 7 October at Winterborne Came Rectory. Quiet burial at Came Church 11 October. Thomas Hardy writes his poem *The Last Signal (Oct.11,1886) A Memory of William Barnes.*

1887 His daughter Lucy Baxter (pseudonym Leader Scott) publishes the biography of her father *The Life of William Barnes. Poet and Philologist.*

1889 4 February bronze statue of Barnes erected at St Peter's church, Dorchester where he had worshipped and preached.

Historic Dates

1805 21 October Battle of Trafalgar. Lord Nelson wounded and died.
1811 George III mentally ill. Prince George appointed Regent.
1815 Battle of Waterloo.
1820 Death of George III. Prince Regent crowned George IV.
1830 George IV dies. William IV crowned King.
1834 Tolpuddle labourers (Tolpuddle Martyrs) transported to Australia for prison term of seven years for attempting to form a Trade Union.
1837 William IV dies. Victoria crowned Queen June, 1837. She was eighteen years of age.
1840 Thomas Hardy born at Higher Bockhampton, Dorchester.
1846 Repeal of the Corn Laws.
1849 Cholera epidemic in the Fordington area of Dorchester. Heroic efforts by Barnes's friend the Rev. Henry Moule to rid the area of disease.
1851 The Great Exhibition. Opened by Queen Victoria in Hyde Park, London on 1 May.
1854 Crimean War (Charge of the Light Brigade).
1868 Gladstone becomes Prime Minister.
1870 Education Act.
1899 Boer War.
1901 Queen Victoria dies.
1902 Coronation of Edward VII postponed. Sir Frederick Treves, Sergeant Surgeon to the King, a pupil of William Barnes, successfully operates on the King for appendicitis.
1983 The William Barnes Society (1983) formed at 6 Lime Close, Dorchester, Dorset DT1 2HQ.

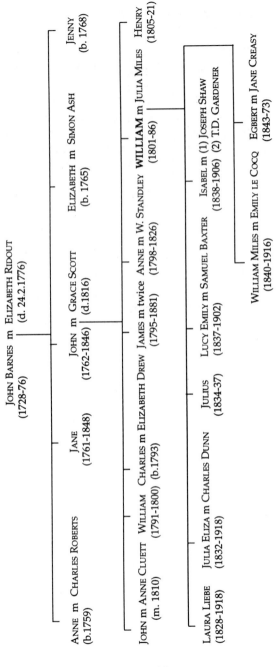

JOHN BARNES m ELIZABETH RIDOUT
(1728-76)   (d. 24.2.1776)

ANNE m CHARLES ROBERTS
(b.1759)

JANE
(1761-1848)

JOHN m GRACE SCOTT
(1762-1846) | (d.1816)

ELIZABETH m SIMON ASH
(b. 1765)

JENNY
(b. 1768)

JOHN m ANNE CLUETT WILLIAM CHARLES m ELIZABETH DREW JAMES m twice ANNE m W. STANDLEY WILLIAM m JULIA MILES HENRY
(m. 1810)   (1791-1800) (b.1793)   (1795-1881)   (1798-1826)   (1801-86)   (1805-21)

LAURA LIEBE
(1828-1918)

JULIA ELIZA m CHARLES DUNN
(1832-1918)

JULIUS
(1834-37)

LUCY EMILY m SAMUEL BAXTER
(1837-1902)

ISABEL m (1) JOSEPH SHAW
(1838-1906) (2) T.D. GARDENER

WILLIAM MILES m EMILY LE COCQ EGBERT m JANE CREASY
(1840-1916)   (1843-73)

10

A map of Dorchester Town showing the Barnes's properties.

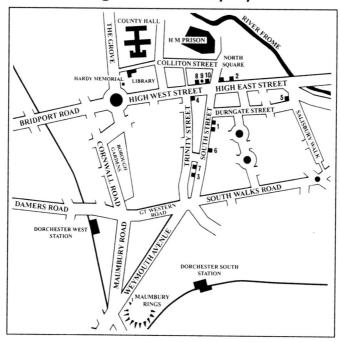

1. *Numbers 5 and 7 South Street. Solicitor Thomas Coombs in 1818 and for many years thereafter owned both these properties using one as his dwelling and the other as his office. Barnes worked here from 1818 to 1823.*

2. *The King's Arms Hotel. Family history has it that it was in the King's Arms Hotel yard that Barnes first saw Miss Julia Miles step from a stagecoach and immediately decided that she would be his future wife.*

3. *Julia Miles lived with her parents James and Isabella Miles in South Street from about 1813 until 1826.*

4. *Possible site of Hazard's Bakers shop where Barnes lodged with his office 'mate' William Gilbert Carey from 1818 to 1823.*

5. *The 'strait-pent house' where Barnes had his first school in Dorchester, 1835-37. It was a bleak and disastrous time for Barnes and his wife. This indicates the possible site.*

6. *His second and most prosperous boarding and day school, Norman's House, 17 South Street, 1838-47.*

7. *His last school, 40 South Street, 1848-62. It was here his beloved wife Julia died. For this and other reasons the school declined.*

8. *Dorset County Museum. Established in October, 1845 Barnes was a founder member and joint secretary.*

9. *Despite vigorous opposition from the Parish Vestry Committee of St Peter's church the statue of William Barnes was eventually unveiled by the Bishop of Salisbury on 4 February 1889.*

10. *St Peter's church. Barnes was at some time church warden, poor steward, sick visitor and preacher here. His youngest daughter Isabel was married here.*

A map of the Dorchester area including Came and Whitcombe.

(See Eric Ricketts's map in Poems Grave and Gay – Weymouth Bookshop ed.)

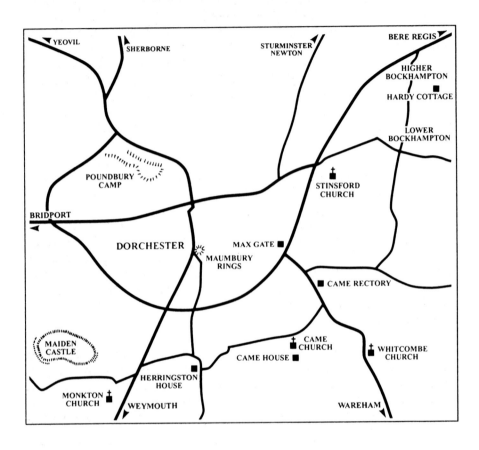

Foresay

Don't be put off by William Barnes's Dorset dialect; not all his poems were written in this form; in fact two volumes were written in what he called National English, ordinary English to you and me. The dialect is relatively easy to read although the art of speaking it is much more difficult. The sound of the words and the musical tones within the reading are a very important part of these poems, particularly the use of the soft Dorset accent of the Blackmore Vale. The Vale accent differs immensely from the harsher tones of both Poole and Weymouth. But when visiting Dorset enjoy what little you can still hear of this dialect as it may soon become extinct. Around 1880, near the end of his life, Barnes had this foreboding when he wrote

> *I have done some little to preserve the speech of our forefathers, but I fear a time will come when it will be scarcely remembered, and none will be found who can speak it with the purity I have heard it spoken in my youth.*

With the movement of people throughout the world and the modern means of communication, accents have become diluted, new words are added from other languages and Barnes's prediction is rapidly becoming true. He wanted a pure language based on Anglo-Saxon, the ancient speech of Britain, a simple language which excluded French and Latin words then used by the aristocracy; a language all could understand and particularly his Dorset parishioners.

It is important to remember that the words in Barnes's poems relate to the nineteenth century and the era of the horse and waggon; many of them are not modern words. However, he published a most useful dictionary on the subject of dialect, *A Glossary of the Dorset Dialect with a Grammar of its Shapening and Wording* and I have appended a brief list of words from this glossary with their meanings.

In the printed word of his dialect poems certain letters are replaced by others so that when the poems are read the phonetics or speech sounds of the words are those of the Dorset dialect. An example is the letter 'z' which replaces the letter 's'. The word sun is printed zun, sight becomes zight, so becomes zo and more often than not written zoo. The letter 'f' is pronounced as 'v'; fall is vall, find is printed vind and far is var. And then there is the use of the letter 'w' often placed in front of the letter 'o'; one is printed as woone, home becomes hwome, old is wold and mwost is most and so on. And to complicate matters 'e' is placed in the middle of a word in front of the letter 'a' so that face becomes feace; glare gleare and mates meates.

Then there is the occasional prefix and suffix. Dorset folk have the habit of using 'a' as a prefix; when you are waiting for something you are 'a-biding' or if walking 'a-foot' or working in a field, 'a-field'. And to add to the mystery they will lengthen and shorten the actual word as they think fit and then add the letters 'en'; glass becomes 'glassen', could not becomes 'cooden', twisted becomes 'twinen'.

The slackness in pronunciation is commonplace in any dialect. In Dorset the letter 'd' is missed at the end of a word so that round becomes roun'; and is an'. The letter 'w' gets similar treatment but at the beginning of a word; within becomes 'ithin; would is 'ould; and the slackness continues with 'ing' becoming 'en'; clinging is clinen; come or coming is comen; hissing becomes hissen.

Particular words often play several parts in the speech as the vocabulary is very limited but these words I'm afraid you will have to try and fathom out for yourself. As an example 'thik' could mean this or that or those. I might or I may is covered by 'mid'; so that a simple translation of ' I might read this book' could be 'I mid read thik girt piece'. With a limited vocabulary the speaker would doubtless not use the word 'book' so reference would be made to a 'great piece' meaning something important and that same term could apply to many other objects.

This man was born and bred – indeed died – in Dorset, rarely moving out of the Wessex area during the whole of his long life. He was a self-taught scholar with deep religious convictions and a passion for education. A gentle man in every sense of the word; full of compassion for the rights of the poor; someone who had the grace never to forget his humble upbringing.

Barnes died at Winterborne Came Rectory, just on the outskirts of Dorchester, on 7 October, 1886 in his eighty-sixth year.

It seems odd that I should tell you of his death even before you know about his life but it is only because I feel that everyone who visits Dorchester should at least try to see his statue. After a great deal of fund raising and commotion, John Wordsworth, the Bishop of Salisbury unveiled the bronze statue on 4 February, 1889. It stands where it always has done during the past century in front of St Peter's church in the old churchyard next to the Dorset County Museum. It was the first public statue ever to be erected in Dorchester.

Barnes's poems are meant to be enjoyed. They are but a small part of his total literary output which includes works on philology, a dictionary of the Dorset dialect, books and papers on economics, art, religion, Ancient Britain and antiquities.

Rev. William Barnes, Dorset parson, poet and schoolmaster. (Dorset County Museum).

MY ORCHA'D IN LINDEN LEA

'Ithin the woodlands, flow'ry gleaded,
By the woak tree's mossy moot
The sheenen grass-bleades, timber-sheaded,
Now do quiver under voot;
An' birds do whissle over head,
An' water's bubblen in its bed,
An' there vor me the apple tree
Do lean down low in Linden Lea.

When leaves that leately wer a-springen
Now do feade 'ithin the copse,
An' painted birds do hush their zingen
Up upon the timber tops;
An' brown-leav'd fruit's a-turnen red,
In cloudless zunsheen, over head,
Wi' fruit vor me, the apple tree
Do lean down low in Linden Lea.

Let other vo'k meake money vaster
In the air o' dark-room'd towns,
I don't dread a peevish measter;
Though no man do heed my frowns,
I be free to goo abrode,
Or teake agean my homeward road
To where, vor me, the apple tree
Do lean down low in Linden Lea. [1]

[Jones: p233]

16

WILLIAM BARNES
The Dorset Poet
1801-1886

Poverty was rife throughout England at the beginning of the nineteenth century and the county of Dorset was no exception. The unrest caused by the French Revolution, the cost of fighting the Napoleonic Wars combined with such economic measures as the Corn Laws had exhausted the wealth of the country as well as its population. The Industrial Revolution was well underway and the labouring classes were soon organising themselves into unions. The small Dorsetshire village of Tolpuddle would in 1834 become the centre of political attention as the Martyrs were found guilty of 'unlawful combination by taking secret oaths' and in consequence were transported to Australia to endure a form of slavery.

Into the small rural community of Bagber in the Blackmore Vale, William Barnes was born on 22 February, 1801 to Grace and John Barnes. John Barnes was a labourer in husbandry who occupied a small farmling called Rush-hay but lived mainly by hiring out his labour and by the free use of the common land. His skills were much the same as those of an ordinary farm worker so that his livelihood was barely above subsistence level. There were already four children in the family when Barnes was born; ultimately six. Some were forced to leave home, others were to die young.

Within the decade, two of Barnes's three elder brothers, John and James, had moved to Portsmouth and joined the fishing fleets which plied the lucrative salt cod trade between England and Newfoundland. Charles Barnes, almost certainly known as Charlie, married Elizabeth Drew, left home, but remained in the Sturminster Newton area as a farm labourer. For some time William's only sister Ann helped their mother keep house as well as working on the farmling but life would not to be easy for her. When their mother died in 1816 Ann was left to look after her father and her two younger brothers William aged fifteen and Henry aged nine.

Apart from the three terms he spent at St John's College, Cambridge, when he was fifty years of age, the only formal education Barnes received was at the Sturminster Newton endowed church school which he left at the age of thirteen.[2] Barnes was an extremely intelligent child who had one great advantage: for the Victorian philanthropist he was the ideal working class boy and they were more than ready to help him. The Rev. James Michel of Sturminster Newton allowed Barnes the use of his library as, at a later date, did the Rev. J.H. Richman of Dorchester. Both these men willingly gave their time to teach him Greek and Latin and the Rev. Richman in particular instructed him on the techniques of writing poetry.

Bagber was a remote Dorset hamlet and in some respects it was an ideal place for this future rural poet to develop. During his childhood and early 'teens he absorbed all the sights and sounds of the countryside in his beloved Blackmore Vale and in later years he would describe them through his dialect poetry. Barnes was a self-taught genius who, despite being socially ambitious, was content to remain a rural schoolmaster and priest throughout his life. A man of simple tastes, full of tenderness and devotion, he was well ahead of his time in both thought and deed and as the first verse of *The Young Rhymer Snubbed* indicates he was definitely a realist.

William Barnes in his youth. An early self portrait when he cherished the hope of a career in art. Notice his shelf of books: 'teachers of the little taught' he called them. (Dorset County Museum).

> To meake up rhymes, my mind wer zoo a-vire
> 'Twer idle work to try to keep me quiet,
> O' meaken rhymes my heart did never tire;
> Though I should never be a gainer by it.
> 'You meake up rhyme!' vo'k zaid, 'why who would buy it?
> Could you write fine enough to please a squire?
> An' rhyme's what plain vo'k woudden much require;
> You'd vind your rhymes would earn but scanty diet,
> An' if I'd any cure vor it, I'm sure I'd try it.'

Around 1814 he started work as a clerk in the office of Mr Thomas Dashwood, a solicitor of Sturminster Newton. Tradition has it that Barnes was sketching in a field, Mr Dashwood saw him, was impressed with the drawing and promptly employed him. This precise early training in a lawyer's office and his keen observation of people and circumstances would stand him in good stead in later life.

Although Barnes left no record of his mother in any of his scrapbooks some of his poems reveal that he was obviously very attached to her so that her death in 1816 was a terrible blow for this fifteen year old boy. Also within a year his employer Mr Dashwood died and Barnes became unemployed. He found a temporary job with a Mr Score of Sturminster Newton but was soon again unemployed. Economic circumstances and the overcrowding of small properties were the prime causes which forced large families to split up but these additional sorrows must have prompted Barnes to leave home. ℞ Throughout his long life he seldom returned to his beloved Blackmore Vale and even on the rare occasions when he did it was only ever a fleeting visit. But his spirit never left the Vale. Some thirty years later when he was well established and living in Dorchester, he bought two fields in Sturminster Newton through his solicitor Henry Dashwood, son of Thomas his original employer.
He records:

1847: This year £200 which I had lent on Mortgage at Sturminster Newton was paid off and I bought Creedman's and Moggs Mead at Sturminster for £360.

It brought him little income but a great deal of happiness.

Leaving a pre-occupied father, a dispirited sister and a desolate younger brother, Barnes moved to Dorchester in June 1818 where he was employed as an engrossing clerk in the office of Mr Thomas Coombs, a solicitor of South Street, Dorchester. Although essentially a country boy, Barnes must have been a very agreeable and presentable young man as not only his 'mate', as he called his office colleague William Carey, but his many companions of those early years in Dorchester remained his friends throughout their lives. One such was a young man of private means named Edward Fuller.

William Carey was slightly older than Barnes and a senior clerk with Thomas Coombs. Barnes and Carey shared lodgings over 'Mr Hazard's Bakers Shop' believed to be at the corner of High West Street and Trinity

Street. Carey was a good and practical friend to Barnes, helping him to apply for various jobs to improve his status and income. As an indication of Barnes's ability he applied for an appointment at Pattison's Bank in Dorchester but 'two sureties each in the sum of £1000' were required. This was a huge and impossible amount of money to raise and despite Carey's pleadings and unsuccessful attempt to get the sureties removed Barnes did not get the job. But it was Carey's advice which would alter the whole course of Barnes's life.

Edward Fuller was different. He was a young gentleman of independent means and it was he who improved the social and intellectual status of Barnes. Joined by Mr and Mrs Zillwood, owners of a bookshop in Dorchester, Fuller and Barnes played in a musical quartet, Barnes being proficient with both the violin and flute. They regularly spoke and corresponded with each other in French and in later life visited each other. If circumstances had allowed, they would have undertaken foreign travel but both Fuller and his wife died from tuberculosis within a short time of each other. They were just forty years of age and had been married for less than two years. In his will Edward Fuller left Barnes a generous legacy of £100. Barnes was moved to write this epitaph for his friend.

TO DEAD FRIENDS

Departed spirits, living far away;
Oh! could ye hear my whispers where ye dwell,
Or could my prayer, like a magic spell,
Bring back your beaming forms to where I stray;
How would I meet you, when the busy day
Had left calm moonlight in the wood and dell,
And talk with you of others, and tell
The joys and sorrows of this breathing clay.

But ye are far away, no more to tread
The busy ways of men, or to be seen
In lonely path, or laughter-sounding room.

A gulf between the living and the dead
Is fix'd for ever, and our Lord has been
Our life of glory only through the tomb.

[Jones: p672]

Julia Miles Barnes. (Courtesy J. Stevens Cox).

Miss Julia Miles was about fourteen years of age when tradition has it that the seventeen year old Barnes saw her stepping from a stagecoach outside the King's Arms Hotel in Dorchester. He instantly fell in love with her and vowed she would be his wife. Julia Miles was the younger of two daughters of Mr and Mrs James Campfield Miles. James Miles was the excise officer for the Dorchester area who, assisted by his eight sons, spent a considerable amount of time chasing smugglers and their contraband along the Dorset coast. Doubtless because his daughter was so young, and possibly due to the artistic nature of Barnes, James Miles was unhappy about their friendship and the few letters and invitations written to Julia by Barnes during this period indicate a secretive courtship.[3] Some letters were delivered by hand to the Miles household obviously in order to save expensive postage but for some reason one or two were posted to Julia at addresses in Dorchester other than the Miles family home. Were his letters being intercepted? Whether this was so, or not, is impossible to prove but Barnes certainly didn't help the situation. As might be expected he was zealous and hard working at his job but he had also been picked out by a group of influential people in Dorchester who gave him considerable support and companionship. But not content with this it was as though he had to prove his manhood and his independence and so at about nineteen years of age he had printed, at his own expense, a slim volume of *Poetical Pieces. By William Barnes.* Printed by G. Clark, High Street, Dorchester, 1820. One of the poems in this booklet was called *Destiny*, a long rambling affair complaining how destiny had ill treated him in his relationship with Julia. Whilst not mentioning Mr and Mrs Miles by name there were obvious implications.

DESTINY [two verses only]

Her fortunate stars had to Julia given,
Of lovers a numerous train,
Who for twelvemonths, or more, had incessantly striven
To win her fair hand – but in vain.
They were all youths of merit, although they were poor,
And to one she'd nigh given her heart;
But her father he lik'd the pecun'ary ore,
Insomuch that in one of his passions he swore
That Julia should ne'er again enter his door,
If to him she her hand should impart.

Her mama urg'd with much assiduity too,
When she thought of becoming a wife,
The advantage of keeping the maxim in view,
That 'gold's the best passport thro' life.'
And she too, like papa, was a little severe
In adverting to Julia's love;
Who, she said, was but just in her seventeenth year,
And had beauty, forsooth, which she'd not the least fear,
Would raise her some day to a much higher sphere,
Than that in which Cyprian could move.

The contents of this poem are not only surprising but spiteful and seem to be completely out of character for the young and sensitive Barnes. His frustration did not justify him being so discourteous, particularly as his booklet was being sold in Dorchester and the inhabitants of any importance were well aware that the poem referred to Mr and Mrs Miles in all but name. And yet he blithely invited Julia to concerts, took her for trips on the river Frome in his little boat and joined her for many strolls through the town 'Walks'. The Miles family appear to have remained aloof from this courtship as there is never any mention of Barnes being invited to tea or to any of their family events. Strangely, and somewhat selfishly, such were his many literary and musical activities in the town that his courtship of Julia took second place to his social life. Yet during this mixed-up period he wrote some delightful sonnets occasionally illustrated with watercolours and, of course, poems to his beloved Julia.

Mr and Mrs James Miles were soon to get some respite from their daughter's suitor. In 1823 Barnes left Dorchester and almost immediately their attitude towards him changed. Barnes was now accepted by the Miles family and he would occasionally make holiday visits to Dorchester but never apparently to their home.

SONNET

The hour of parting is arriv'd at last.
I now must go, and ere we meet again
The woods will bend with many a wint'ry blast,
And streams will swell by gloomy storms of rain;
From lofty mountains, over vale and plain,
Full many an evening shadow will be cast;
And many a laden vessel o'er the main
Within its quiet haven shall have past.

And many a tongue unknown to thee shall talk
To me, and I shall look on many a face
That wears a smile, or turns away to weep.
And I shall stray in many a lonely walk,
And, turning to my cheerless resting place,
Wear out the night with longer care than sleep.

[Jones: p56]

William Gilbert Carey had been educated at Mere in Wiltshire. The headmaster of his old school had recently died and Carey suggested that Barnes should take over the school. Quite why Barnes should suddenly change his profession is difficult to imagine as he had no experience as a teacher although he had a considerable knowledge of languages and mathematics as well as music and art. He must have been desperate to improve his status even to the extent of getting away from Dorchester. On a bleak day in January, 1823 he left for Mere. In his Notes [4] he wrote:

> So armed with the learning which I had won, and on hearing, as it were in my mind, the words 'doctus a docendo', I went at the age of twenty-two and took up a school which had dropped through the death of its Master, at Mere by Gillingham, though it was in Wiltshire; a school of which my office-mate at Dorchester (Mr Carey) had been a pupil. It was to be his 'most mind-fitting way of life'.

Clearly to change professions would not be easy but to add to his problems Barnes arrived in Mere to find the school was no longer in existence.

However he managed to rent the Old Cross Loft which was on the floor above the Market House in the town centre but unfortunately the room also housed the town clock which regularly struck the hour. Although running the school occupied most of his time he still continued to study a vast range of subjects which in later years would help him to write and publish several school textbooks. Rarely was he able to visit Julia but he regularly corresponded with her and even occasionally sent her love poems.

TO J...

My Julia! 'tis sweet to think
How once, in boyhood's sweet delight,
I wandered by the river's brink,
Or under trees of wond'rous height;
When, far, in fields thou knowest not,
I roved beneath the summer sun,
And rested in the lonely cot
When all my daily sports were done.
Sweeter in memory, when past,
Are all our joys than while they last.

[Jones: p52]

Mere was a declining market town so that it was with difficulty that Barnes managed to recruit and maintain sufficient pupils to give him a meagre living. The first four years of lonely bachelorhood with his dog as his only companion were suddenly transformed. He was offered and rented Chantry House at Mere and with undue haste for one so serious and academic Barnes rushed to Nailsea near Bristol where the Miles family now lived. He obtained approval from her father to marry Julia, collected a special licence and on 27 July, 1827 married Miss Julia Miles, 'Spinster, of the age of twenty-one upwards', at the parish church of Holy Trinity, Nailsea. He then returned to Mere to open a day-and-boarding school at Chantry House the whole adventure taking place virtually within the week. Barnes noted 'In 1827 I took Chantry House at Mere, and brought home my most loveworthy and ever beloved wife Julia Miles and then took boarders'.[5]

These years at Mere were to be some of the happiest of his life. Barnes was twenty-six years of age and Julia twenty-two when they began their idyllic married life and owners of an academy. Chantry House, which is still occupied, is only separated from St Michael's church by small walled gardens and with its 'six or seven rooms above stairs, a large Dining Room with a

Chantry House, Mere, c.1830. William and Julia Barnes married in 1827 and from that date until 1835 they kept Chantry House as a school for boys and girls. This house prompted Barnes to write the poems On Leaving a Garden *and* Linden Lea.

Parlour and Kitchens etc., below' [6] it was an ideal property for a boarding school. It was rented to them at '20 guineas per annum' [£21].

Despite his shyness Barnes was a natural teacher and throughout his life he possessed the desire and ability to impart knowledge. But he was no administrator and this aspect of school life he conveniently left to his wife. The young and inexperienced Julia not only undertook teaching but was also responsible for the feeding and accommodation of the boarders as well as that of her own family. Throughout the years it was she who took over the onerous business of running their various schools and it was her financial acumen that contributed to the success of the schools and her husband's career.

To his delight this change of status from bachelor to married man brought Barnes a sudden increase in social activities and with responsibilities shared, particularly those which absolved him from meeting parents and recruiting scholars, it allowed this timid man to come into his own. With what little time he had to spare he began writing poetry and prose and, like his other activities, it became part of his daily life. He read widely. It was a period of pleasurable consolidation.

The seclusion of Chantry House allowed him to become more domesticated so that growing his own produce and the maintenance of his garden was one of his joys. To obtain further income he undertook engravings to a professional standard [7] and added to his skills by turning his own furniture on a home-made lathe, producing trinkets in silver for his wife and providing endless hand-made toys for his children.

Such was his knowledge that during this period, around 1830, he became a lifelong contributor to both the *Dorset County Chronicle* and the *Gentleman's Magazine*. His contributions included observations on history, religion, philology, the Greek, Latin and French languages as well as advice on practical subjects. He was extremely interested in the theatre and began to write plays but because of his awareness and retention of the sights and sounds of the Bagber countryside he was constantly drawn towards writing poetry particularly dialect poetry.

> *I saw all the dear scenes and well remembered events and beloved faces of youth all distinctly before me, and all I had to do was to write them down ... the thoughts and words came of themselves.*[8]

His first dialect poem was written in the late autumn of 1833 and published in *The Dorset County Chronicle* on 2 January, 1834; the title *Rusticus Dolens, or Inclosures of Common. A Dorsetshire Eclogue in the Dorset Dialect, by a Native of the County*. Barnes was scornful of the injustices caused by enclosing the common land and its subsequent effect upon the poor but as his attitude could be construed as being political he lacked the confidence to add his name as the author of the poem. At a much later date he wrote under the pseudonym of 'Dilettante'.[9] In theory the common land was enclosed in order to make farming more efficient and so produce more and cheaper food but in practice it was simply given to the wealthier landowners and the free use of the common was taken away from the poor.

Although he raised several questions of a political and social nature Barnes never really described the conditions under which the Dorsetshire peasantry lived. He ably details some of the agricultural upheaval of the 1830s in his eclogues *The Unioners, The Common A-Took In* and *The New Poor Laws* but seemed blissfully unaware of the plight in 1834 of the Tolpuc Martyrs. In some respects he was guilty of providing his Victorian pu with the innocent scenes of rustic beauty and simplicity they longed to Robert Young ['Rabin Hill', 1811-1908], a contemporary dialect poet also from Sturminster Newton and a friend of Barnes was much nearer the mark with his descriptions of flogging, drunkenness, wretched housing and abject poverty. Barnes, because of his sensitivity, his shyness and with his deep-rooted religious beliefs could possibly only see the purer aspects of his surroundings. His faith in the goodness of mankind and his God was paramount.

The first of his three volumes of *Poems of Rural Life* appeared in 1844. Other volumes of Dialect and National English poems followed in later years, totalling nearly 1000 poems. These poems strikingly describe the poverty of the farm labourer and the work and limited pastimes of Dorset country folk; they deal with nature, injustice and innocence, love and faith and, always important to Barnes, self-help and hope. For their description of country life during the early part of the nineteenth century they are considered among the best in literature and Barnes is undeniably a leading English provincial dialect poet. His well-drawn verse and technical expertise brought him to the attention of poets of his generation such as Tennyson, Palgrave, Gosse and Patmore, and his much younger neighbour Thomas Hardy.

As Julia and William prospered so did their family. But all was not sweetness and light. On 25 November, 1828 their first daughter was born and christened Laura Liebe to be followed by Julia Eliza christened on 11 February, 1832. There was then a family silence; not even a whisper; a secret, a well kept secret. Sometime during 1834 their first son Julius was born and this fact was only discovered in 1965 some 150 years after the event. Later research has verified that Julius was baptised on 30 June, 1834 at Nailsea near Bristol and was buried in All Saints churchyard, Dorchester on 17 May, 1837 being just three years of age. Barnes and his wife, as well as their daughters Laura and Julia who were old enough to witness this tragedy, expunged all memory of their son and brother. It was as though he never existed. Except maybe through a poem written by his father;

THE MOTHER'S DREAM

I'd a dream to-night
As I fell asleep, –
Oh! the touching sight
Makes me still to weep, –
Of my little lad
Gone to leave me sad;
Aye, the child I had,
But was not to keep.

As in heaven high
I my child did seek,
There, in train, came by
Children fair and meek;
Each in lily white,
With a lamp alight;
Each was clear to sight,
But they did not speak.

Then a little sad
Came my child in turn;
But the lamp he had,
Oh! it did not burn;
He, to clear my doubt,
Said, half turned about,
'Your tears put it out;
Mother, never mourn.'

[Jones: p814]

Despite his own problems Barnes, now in his early thirties, was very aware of the plight of the poor. It is difficult to believe but the economic effects of the Napoleonic Wars were still being felt in Britain during the 1830s. The price of wheat, the staple food of the working classes, was at its highest during 1815 but with the end of hostilities and good harvests during the ensuing years the price had more than halved. This gave farmers the excuse to reduce the pay of their labourers who were already living below subsistence level and the effect upon the Barnes family, who were just managing to survive in the Blackmore Vale, was catastrophic. Charlie Roberts, an uncle and a once prosperous man, was evicted from his smallholding and

Barnes's father John fared little better. It was this poverty, combined with the enclosure of land and the introduction of farm machinery that caused unrest among the agricultural labourers. Agitation throughout Wiltshire and Dorset by a mysterious 'Captain Swing' gave rise to the illegal burning of crops and damage to farm machinery. To the dismay of the country's landowners Trades Unions were being formed among the working classes which culminated, in 1834, with the deportation to Australia of the Tolpuddle Martyrs for seven years. Mere was not exempt from the agricultural depression and the consequential results upon its inhabitants added to Barnes's difficulties. The poverty within the area meant fewer pupils attending his school and more parents failing to pay their school fees. As so often happens there was a saving grace as this enforced idleness gave Barnes the excuse to undertake his work and his hobbies within the confines of Chantry House. His wife was more than aware of the situation and Mr C.J. Wallis,[10] a one-time pupil at the academy, reported her comments: 'Mr Barnes, you are burying your talents in this poor, out-of the-way place.' On 26 June, 1835 he and his family left Chantry House, Mere for 'a straight-up penthouse' in Durngate Street, Dorchester.[11]

Dorchester was a thriving market town. With such prosperous inhabitants Barnes was of the opinion there would be better prospects for him and his type of academy in the county town. He was right. They both knew Dorchester well, the place held happy youthful memories for them and for the shy Barnes the surroundings were more socially acceptable than Mere. And with a growing family they needed the money. Regrettably the two years they sojourned in the Durngate Street schoolhouse was a time of sadness. Overcrowding, sickness and even death was always present. The school certainly flourished but it was a barren period for Barnes who had little time for his poetry and prose. He missed the quietness of Chantry House with its stream and garden. Time was scarce and inspiration was lacking.

To add to their problems Julia's father, James Campfield Miles, was killed in a road accident and Mrs Miles with two of her sons, joined the Barnes family in Durngate Street. The schoolhouse was already full to overflowing with 10 or more boarders, two servants, a trainee schoolmaster and at least 25 day-boys. Barnes, his wife, and their three children were also in residence and to add to the confusion and numbers, on 21 January, 1837 their fourth child Lucy Emily was born. In May of the same year, with silent assent, they buried their son Julius in All Saints churchyard, Dorchester to

South Street, Dorchester, 1859. This property was on the west side of South Street and would have been roughly opposite Barnes's second and most prosperous school at 17 South Street. Barnes was still living in South Street, at No. 40 when this photograph was taken. He probably knew the 'stove pipe' hatted gentleman and certainly would have recognised the unmade road. (Dorset County Museum).

be followed almost immediately by one of Mrs Miles's sons who had died from tuberculosis. They decided to move house and school. On 22 January, 1838 Barnes opened his prestigious school at Norman's House, 17 South Street, Dorchester.[12]

Sometime in 1838 another daughter, Isabel, was born to be followed by a son William Miles Barnes on 19 March, 1840.

With between 40 and 50 students, many of whom were boarders, Norman's House school was not only financially successful but was thriving due in no small measure to his wife Julia. It was under these stimulating circumstances that Barnes extended his scholarly activities. The wide range of subjects he taught not only catered for the academic student but also covered practical skills. Well ahead of his time in teaching methods, he was renowned for his early morning lectures, his field studies and the preparation, in obscure languages, of students for Military Academies and the Overseas Civil Service. Decimal coinage, the use of a phonetic alphabet for reading and a completely modern approach to experimental sciences, including navigation, all had his enthusiastic support and yet he continued to teach all the basic subjects including religion, music and even the relatively new game of cricket. He published his own text books and maintained a gentle but simple discipline within his school whilst establishments such as Eton and Winchester had to call in the army to quell drunken students. His teaching vocation lasted nearly forty years, from 1823 to 1862, and his outstanding ability as the master and owner of relatively small provincial academies is best illustrated by the lives and careers of some of his pupils. Sir Frederick Treves, Surgeon to Queen Victoria and King Edward VII; Judge Tolbort, Indian Civil Service; Rev. Professor Walter Lock, Warden, Keble College, Oxford; Joseph Clark, R.A., Victorian artist; Rev. O.P. Cambridge, naturalist; Sir Edward Pearce Edgcombe, banker, lawyer; as well as many other national and local dignitaries.

Such was his mental energy that not all his academic capacity was confined to his school. This great desire for learning was kindled in his humble home at Bagber with books freely provided by the local clergy and as he grew older Barnes's ability displayed itself in a wide range of publications; *An investigation of the Laws of Case in Language* (1840); *An Arithmetical and Commercial Dictionary* (1840); *Se Gefylsta (The Helper): An Anglo-Saxon Delectus* (1849); *A Philological Grammar* (1854)[13]; *Views of Labour and Gold* (1859), *Roots and Stems of English as a Teutonic Tongue* (1862) and *A Grammar and Glossary of the Dorset Dialect* (1863); *An Outline of English Speech-Craft* (1878). This list of books, many of more than 300 pages long, is not comprehensive and when added to the booklets, pamphlets and magazine articles he wrote, and his poems, points to an extraordinary talent.

The prosperous Mrs Julia Barnes was thirty-eight years of age when her sixth and last child Egbert was born in 1843. The middle-class schoolmaster was now listed under 'Gentry' in the Dorchester *Kelly's Directory* of 1844. It was an exciting time for the whole family.

Even more exciting for the 'Durnovarians' [14] was the fact that Dorchester was about to be linked to the Southern as well as the Western railway systems. But there was a snag. The railway lines were to be laid through

Poundbury Roman Camp and Maumbury Rings, the magnificent Roman amphitheatre. Barnes, an antiquarian and ecologically minded person, was a founder and first Secretary of the Dorset Natural History and Antiquarian Field Club.[15] Assisted by many friends, he was instrumental in persuading the railway companies to divert their railway lines and thus saved these monuments which are in their original condition even to this day.

In 1844, ostensibly to discuss future plans with his publisher, Barnes made his first tentative but still tedious coach and train journey to London and was the guest of the Honourable Mrs Caroline Norton, one of the three gifted sisters of Richard Brinsley Sheridan of Frampton Court, Dorchester. In some respects the visit was not a success and although they remained on friendly terms he was not at ease among high society. Mrs Norton so admired Barnes's poems that she arranged a poetry reading by him, in London, which was to be attended by Queen Victoria. However, sickness and Mrs Norton's involvement in a scandalous court case involving Lord Melbourne caused the event to be cancelled. Despite her support there was a complete lack of interest in Barnes's *Poems of Rural Life in the Dorset Dialect* when they were first published in 1844 but after about three years the climate changed and reprints and new editions were published in 1847, 1862 and 1866. Other collections and editions followed including two volumes where all his poems are written in National English. Throughout this century various reprints have been undertaken as well as anthologies by Thomas Hardy, the Rev. W. Miles Barnes, Geoffrey Grigson, John Drinkwater, Christopher Ricks, Andrew Motion and others.

This solitary rural poet with his acute observations was able to intertwine his quiet Dorset humour with his love for mankind. Dorset folk, nature, Christian love and faith, his beloved Blackmore Vale are all portrayed in his poems and so he leaves an unsurpassed record of life in rural England during the early part of the nineteenth century.

Because of his numerous talents, and with the support of his wife, he was able to undertake many other pursuits outside his teaching career and his writing. He was a preacher, a church warden and a sick visitor; held poetry readings, lectured throughout the South of England on all sorts of subjects to all sorts of societies; was a philologist and archaeologist.

Religion was always uppermost in Barnes's mind. He was a practical as well as a practising Christian, and there was always a latent desire to take holy orders. At that time it was possible to obtain a degree at St John's College, Cambridge on a part-time basis; indeed, higher education of the poor was one of the founding conditions of this liberal college. Barnes was accepted 'on the books' as a 'ten year man' which meant that during that period he had to undertake a course of study, at home, to be followed by three term's attendance at St John's for a series of examinations.

SABBATH LAYS! 1844
No.2
'Teach us to pray.'
Luke, Chap.11,v.1

O Lord we pray not as we ought;
We pray in word but not in thought.
Our hearts are dull and cold; we kneel
And tell of wants we do not feel.
But warm our chilly hearts of clay,
And teach us, teach us how to pray.

We ask for pow'r, we ask for gold,
We ask what mercy must withhold;
We ask for life, and earthly bliss,
And fail because we ask amiss.
But take our blindness, Lord, away,
And teach us, teach us how to pray.

And while we thus in folly lift
Our voice to ask some baneful gift,
How coldly, Father, do we call
To Thee for Grace, Thou all in all.
O take our ignorance away,
And teach us, teach us how to pray.
[Jones: p584]

His studies for a divinity degree combined with his lay activities at St Peter's church, Dorchester made Barnes an obvious candidate to become a Church of England clergyman and on 28 February, 1847 he was ordained Deacon and appointed Stipend Curate of Winterborne Whitcombe church, near Dorchester, at an annual fee of £13. During the same year he moved his growing family and expanding school across the road into the Hawkins

Winterborne Whitcombe church. Barnes was appointed Stipend Curate here in 1847. (Dorset County Museum).

property at 40 South Street and promptly built a huge classroom and play-room in the garden to cater for his many day students and boarders. He was now at the height of his teaching career. Fitfully during 1847 to 1850 he attended St John's College, Cambridge to undertake examinations and to preach sermons before members of the faculty. He obtained his Divinity Degree in October 1850.

Whilst his fame grew so his wife's health appeared to decline. As though to make up for his absence at Cambridge, and possibly apprehensive of the future, he decided to take Julia and two of his daughters, Laura and Julia, to the 1851 Exhibition,[16] the 'Great Exhibition at the Crystal Palace', in Hyde Park, London. The visit lasted four days and was a resounding success. And to complete the joyful occasion there was the chance meeting at the exhibition with the overweight Job Rose, an old friend and miller from the Blackmore Vale. This happy event gave Barnes the opportunity to write his poem *John Bloom in Lon'on, (All true)* [Jones: p473] which records the impossible task of the bulky Bloom, 'a halfstarv'd Do'set man', trying to squeeze himself into a narrow London horse cab in order to get to the exhibition.

Regretfully Bloom, or Job Rose, 'he wer twice too wide vor thik there door' and so had to walk.

The autumn of 1851 was disastrous. Measles spread throughout the school and affected the family as well as the pupils. The cholera epidemic of 1849 which had started in the Fordington area of Dorchester was never really eradicated and kindred illnesses erupted throughout the town. Barnes became ill and his wife dutifully nursed him. At the beginning of 1852 Julia's health suddenly deteriorated and in order to be with his wife Barnes resigned his minor living as Curate of Winterborne Whitcombe. Despite seeking the highest medical advice it was to no avail when it was discovered that she had been suffering from 'an ulcer of the breast' for some time.

A GUILIA

Ah me! the days glide hastily away,
Although, to mourning, they seem to me but slow;
And I shall soon behold the fatal day,
With whose departing splendour I must go
And leave the idol of my heart in woe,
Or follow her, where she has led the way
Into the silence, where we may not know
The sighs of grief, or laughter of the gay.

And shall I first from mortal life depart,
And leave my dearest Guilia here behind?
Or wilt thou fly from me? Ah! who can tell
But thou art now so dear unto my heart,
That wert thou gone from me, I could not find
A joy without thee: this I know full well.

[Jones: p59]

Julia Miles Barnes died at 40 South Street, Dorchester on 21 June, 1852 at eleven thirty in the morning. Barnes wrote in his scrapbook for 1852:[17]
June 21. A day of sorrow and beginning of a train of sorrows - At half
after eleven o'clock in the morning, my great loss.
I took my sadness to constant work, out of school, as well as in it.

Julia Barnes was buried in St Peter's churchyard which is now the paved area in front of the church and where the statue of her husband William Barnes stands. Her grave is unmarked.

35

Parental guidance and the expense of raising his four daughters and two sons were now his sole responsibility and weighed heavily upon him. Barnes was completely lost without his 'beloved Julia' and for this and other reasons his successful academy began to fail and with it his financial status. He attempted to improve his position by applying for various teaching posts both in and away from Dorchester. Years earlier the situation of headmaster of the Dorchester Grammar School became vacant and Barnes applied for the job but this bewildered soul was to fall foul of the Establishment when, despite considerable local support, the 'feoffees' [trustees] of the school decided not appoint him.

With the death of their mother, Barnes's eldest daughter Laura, twenty-three years of age, was the natural successor to take over all family responsibilities including running the boarding school. She never married and acted as servant and housekeeper to her father until he died. Her sisters Julia and Lucy married and lived permanently in Florence, Italy. Lucy Barnes Baxter [pseudonym Leader Scott] was the author of several books. She entertained and arranged the extensive visit of Mr and Mrs Thomas Hardy to Italy in 1887 and it was in that year that she published the biography of her father, Barnes having died in 1886. Their sister Isabel married twice, her first husband dying young and leaving her a considerable fortune. Barnes's eldest son, the Rev. William Miles Barnes, a caring person with a deep interest in music, was Rector of Winterborne Monkton church, Dorchester for some forty-two years. Egbert, the youngest child, was apprenticed at the Swindon Railway Works and qualified as an engineer. He died aged thirty-one years whilst working on the construction of the new underground railway system in London.

After 1852, out of necessity, Barnes began to re-shape his life. Despite his shyness he was a progressive man well ahead of his time in both social and educational opinions. Such was his generous attitude towards his fellow man that he would prefer to do menial tasks himself rather than ask his servants to undertake them. All the time his wife was alive he still commanded respect in Dorchester and as the owner of a reputable academy he was considered as someone with Tory affiliations. Whether this sudden change of circumstance due to the death of his wife made him focus his thoughts is difficult to verify but his latent attitude hardened to the extent of publishing his social and quasi-political views. Indeed if his writings are to be believed he was already 'Liberal' in his politics, possibly even a Christian Socialist, although doubtless he would have denied the latter. The truth is that his struggle against poverty in his early years, as well as his determined attempt to become educated, had left their mark. The tediousness of obtaining his degree as a 'ten year man' and then possibly being considered an educated layman as distinct from an academic must have rankled, particularly when he applied for other appointments.

This frame of mind quietly manifested itself in the early 1830s when he first began to write his dialect poetry in which he dealt with the need for social reform in favour of the labouring poor. He became more adventurous many years later, albeit anonymously, when in 1848 he published *Humilis Domus* a book which dealt with the life and social conditions of the poor particularly those living in Dorsetshire. Within the decade he published *Labour and Gold*, originally a series of lectures he had given in Dorchester, in which he asserted his social and economic views based on the theory that 'labour is the basis of wealth'. It was not a popular stand to take in a little market town like Dorchester which was full of high Tories.

Whilst his economic theories were basic and straight forward, with the occasional oddity such as support for a Christian redistribution of wealth, his literary views were quite radical. He wanted a people's language, a Saxon English which all could understand, particularly the country folk who were his neighbours and who later made up the majority of his church congregation. At the same time he championed country dialects which were then considered to be the language of the poor and the ignorant. The middle-class folk of Dorchester, many uneducated, suddenly realised that this schoolmaster was alternatively teaching their sons to be educated gentlemen and at the same time publishing poems in the Dorset dialect. And to add to their dismay, Barnes began to extend his radical attitude of treating all men as equal by giving free courses of lectures to working men at Mechanics' Institutes and in his desire to educate the poor he also started a free Library-Museum based in Dorchester eventually to become the Dorset County Museum. Nor were their material wants forgotten when he formed the Dorchester Mutual Improvement Society for 'the advancement of the poor'. As might be expected Barnes's popularity with the tradesfolk of Dorchester declined as his own financial problems forced him to curtail business activities with them. He became inward-looking, even more independent, and in some ways misunderstood and pitied.

During 1861 instead of the usual clamour of boarders there was relative silence within Barnes's academy. The national census of that year records

South Street, Dorchester, 1868. By now Barnes was living in Winterborne Came Rectory. He walked into Dorchester for shopping and to set his watch by that of the Town Hall clock and 'London time'. The building immediately on the right is the Dorchester Grammar School, then Napper's Mite with its clock, a house, and then Barnes's School at 17 South Street, just off the photograph. (Dorset County Museum).

that at 40 South Street there were just seven boarders in residence and Barnes's humiliation was nearly complete. Within a year his classrooms were empty, his school and his teaching career had closed. During these difficult times Barnes suffered a combination of the irony of fate and poetic justice. The day his school closed, *The Times* newspaper published the results of the Indian Civil Service Examination, a national entrance examination which if passed guaranteed a career of power, order, and stability. One of Barnes's pupils, Thomas William Hooper Tolbort, came first in the list of successful candidates in the British Isles and Barnes was inundated with requests from wealthy parents throughout Britain for places in his now defunct school. Another former pupil, Captain Lionel Dawson-Damer graciously came to his aid and offered Barnes the living, which included the Rectory, at Winterborne Came church just on the outskirts of Dorchester.

Winterborne Came church. At the church service held in February of each year to commemorate the life and works of the Rev. William Barnes flowers are laid on his grave which lies on the extreme left of this photograph. (Dorset County Museum).

The Rev. William Barnes had at last found security, solace, and some recognition for the vast amount of endeavour he had put into his vocation.

A new and satisfying life lay ahead of him when, aged sixty-one years, he became a gentle Victorian country parson with all the time in the world to read, to write and to minister to his parishioners. For the next twenty-four years he lived in Came Rectory, a comfortable thatched property with fine gardens and within easy walking distance of Dorchester. Under these ideal conditions he continued to write poetry, countless articles for magazines and further books particularly on philology. His poems were again popular and he republished them in various collections adding new work as he thought appropriate. Thus he came to the attention of such men of letters as Tennyson, Gosse, Palgrave, Kilvert and his neighbour Thomas Hardy from nearby Max Gate so that Came Rectory and its venerable occupier became a place of pilgrimage.

Winterborne Came Rectory, 1882. From left to right: Constance Barnes; Harry Gardner, brother of Isabel Barnes's second husband Tom Gardner; William Barnes seated; Arthur Barnes on donkey; Annette Gardner wife of Harry; Ethel Barnes; William Miles Barnes, Barnes's son; Laura Barnes, Barnes's daughter. Constance, Arthur and Ethel were the children of Miles Barnes. (Dorset County Museum).

In the simplicity of his pastoral living, and his final career, Barnes had the love and support of his family; his son Willie was Rector of the next parish; his eldest daughter Laura cared for him until he died. A year before his death Barnes was already a sick man and as he lay in bed hearing the noise of the gate closing behind his visitors he dictated this, his last dialect poem, to his daughter Laura.

THE GEATE A-VALLEN TO

*In the zunsheen ov our zummers
Wi' the hay time now a-come,
How busy wer we out a-vield
Wi' vew a-left at hwome,
When waggons rumbled out ov yard*

40

Red wheeled, wi' body blue,
As back behind 'em loudly slamm'd
The geate a-vallen to.

Drough daysheen ov how many years
The geate ha' now a-swung
Behind the veet o' vull-grown men
An' vootsteps ov the young.
Drough years o' days it swung to us
Behind each little shoe,
As we tripped lightly on avore
The geate a-vallen to.

In evenen time o' starry night
How mother zot at hwome,
An' kept her bleazen vire bright
Till father should ha' come,
An' how she quicken'd up an' smiled
An' stirred her vire anew,
To hear the trampen ho'ses' steps
An' geate a-vallen to.

There's moon-sheen now in nights o' fall
When leaves be brown vrom green,
When, to the slammen o' the geate,
Our Jenny's ears be keen,
When the wold dog do wag his tail,
An' Jean could tell to who,
As he do come in drough the geate,
The geate a-vallen to.

An' oft do come a saddened hour
When there must goo away
One well-beloved to our heart's core,
Vor long, perhaps vor aye:
An' oh! it is a touchen thing
The loven heart must rue.
To hear behind his last farewell
The geate a-vallen to.

[Jones: p928]

Rev. William Barnes in old age. (Dorset County Museum).

Barnes died on 7 October, 1886 at Came Rectory, Dorchester in his eighty-sixth year. With unpretentious rural dignity he was buried on 11 October in the churchyard of his Winterborne Came church from where he had ministered to his flock for the previous twenty-four years. The handful of people who attended his funeral reflected his true companions in life. Of the many poets who visited him in his old age and sang his praises only two attended: Francis Palgrave and Thomas Hardy. The rest of the mourners consisting of those with whom he had so much empathy, the villagers and children of his parish.

Thomas Hardy was moved to write this poem.

THE LAST SIGNAL
(Oct. 11, 1886)
A memory of William Barnes

Silently I footed by an uphill road
That led from my abode to a spot yew-boughed;
Yellowly the sun sloped low down to westward,
And dark was the east with cloud.

Then, amid the shadow of that livid sad east,
Where the light was least, and a gate stood wide,
Something flashed the fire of the sun that was facing it,
Like a brief blaze on that side.

Looking hard and harder I knew what it meant –
The sudden shine sent from the livid east scene;
It meant the west mirrored by the coffin of my friend there,
Turning to the road from his green,

To take his last journey forth – he who in his prime
Trudged so many a time from that gate athwart the land!
Thus a farewell to me he signalled on his grave-way,
As with a wave of his hand.

Winterborne-Came Path.[18]

Barnes was a curious mixture of a man, one who could live in and record the past with consummate ease and yet was so advanced in his thinking, such a polymath, that he was ahead of his time. The past was his dream

Statuette of Rev. William Barnes. This is how Dorchester folk would have remem-
bered William Barnes; shovel hat, blanket shawl, hedgerow stick and hand made
shoes. Roscoe Mullins produced two statuettes as prototypes for a larger statue.
The one accepted is of the venerable clergyman with beard and bowed head. This
one of the vigorous octogenarian was rejected. (Dorset County Museum).

world, the present seemed to hold very little for him other than the great desire to work, to record and to teach. Even after death the contrasting aspects of his life continued. The paucity of attendance at his funeral was soon outweighed by the formation of a memorial committee, moved to action after a poor start by John Wordsworth, Bishop of Salisbury. Almost immediately at least 90 dignitaries clamoured to be appointed. With great debate they erected Dorchester's first statue in the town centre in the precinct of St Peter's church. The famous Edwardian surgeon Sir

Frederick Treves, yet another of Barnes's pupils, summed up 'this tardy act of grace' when he recalled in his article in the *Dorset Year Book*, 1915-1916, 'the folk of Dorchester ignored him while he (Barnes) lived and only honoured him when he had passed beyond the sound of their applause'.

Even today that imbalance needs to be adjusted and the hope is that once again Dorset folk will come to appreciate and then fully acknowledge the extraordinary intellectual power of their own scholar, William Barnes, the Dorset Poet, Parson and Schoolmaster.

Statue of William Barnes by Roscoe Mullins, in the old churchyard outside St Peter's church Dorchester. (Dorset County Library).

Notes

1. This popular poem was set to music by Dr Ralph Vaughan Williams.

2. The endowed school is now The William Barnes First School. 'Mr. Dashwoods house' is still occupied and is opposite the school.

3. Correspondence in the Barnes collection at the Dorset County Museum. See also *The Love Poems and Letters of William Barnes and Julia Miles*, Charlotte Lindgren, Dorset Record Society, 1986.

4. The Barnes collection, Dorset County Museum.

5. *William Barnes, The Schoolmaster* by Trevor W. Hearl, M.A. p41.

6. Letter to Julia Miles from Barnes dated 21 March, 1827.

7. See *William Barnes. The Dorset Engravings*, Laurence Keen and Charlotte Lindgren, DNHAS, Dorset County Museum, 1986.

8. Around 1818, the Rev. H. J. Richman, Headmaster, Dorchester Grammar School, almost certainly in a benevolent capacity, explained to Barnes how poetry works. Barnes had no formal training in the subject.

Richman suffered great privations whilst a student at Eton and in consequence did not believe in corporal punishment, an unusual attitude in those days. He was a brilliant teacher, highly emotional, and certainly influenced Barnes's teaching methods. Apparently he warmed his watch before placing it in his waistcoat pocket in case he should catch cold.

9. *Brewer's Dictionary of Phrase and Fable*: 'Dilettante (Italian): an amateur of the fine arts, in opposition to a professor'. *Oxford English Dictionary*: 'a person who dabbles in a subject for his own pleasure'.

10. C. J. Wallis, 'The early manhood of William Barnes, the Dorset Poet', *Gentleman's Magazine*, July 1888.

11. The property and its address have yet to be identified.

12. Opposite the General Post Office, South Street, Dorchester.

13. Barnes notes: 'Grounded upon English and formed from a comparison of more than sixty languages'.

14. Durnovarian: a person who lives or comes from Dorchester. A Roman name.

15. The Dorset County Museum, Dorchester

16. After the cessation of World War Two and in order to raise morale in a much bombed and starving Britain, a 'Festival of Britain' was held in 1951 to show all facets of British life and industry. It was also to celebrate the centenary of the 1851 Great Exhibition. A first edition of Barnes's poems was included in the 1951 London Exhibition.

17. Scrapbook 2, Page 17. Dorset County Museum.

18. *Collected Poems of Thomas Hardy*, New York, Macmillan, 1946, p.444.

Aftersay

I wish I knew more about poetry. I have tried to read *How Poetry Works* by Phillip Davies Roberts [a Penguin publication] but with limited success on my part. How Barnes at such an early age was able to create poetry as well as master the technical skills is difficult to imagine; it is a measure of his greatness that he did so.

I would like to think that you will enjoy and continue to enjoy reading Barnes's poems and to this end the following comments may be of assistance.

You don't have to be one of 'we Do'sets' to understand his poems. Thousands of Dorset folk are unaware that Barnes even existed and this was one of the reasons for forming the William Barnes Society in Dorchester in 1983. He started writing his dialect poems from about 1830 the poems prior to that date, and a few after that date, being in National English. It was as late as 1844 that *Poems of Rural Life in the Dorset Dialect* were first published and as they all relate to his youth in the Blackmore Vale it took from 1818, when he left the Vale, to 1844 for anything to come to fruition. But time did not dim his observations and his poems are considered to be some of the best descriptions of rural life at the turn of the nineteenth century.

For many people the word pictures he produces and the music of the dialect are enough. Some would argue that Barnes is excessive with his sentimentality as well as his rural humour and so tends to put his characters in a poor light. But that was, and still is, Dorset humour; he was not laughing at their country bumpkin ways but he was laughing with them. When Barnes was a boy life was not just hard it was cruel and it was as cruel for him as it was for a farm labourer and in consequence each respected the other. You may feel that nowadays his ethos of 'God and the Squire will provide' is outdated but there is still a great deal of commonsense in many of his poems. Read the poem *The Leane*. It was written about 150 years ago and yet the 'green' content is as relevant today as it was then. What a wonderful description – a 'travellen chap' – of an unscrupulous city property dealer trying to buy up lanes, droves and 'drongways' to prevent their free use by villagers.

Rhythm and rhyming. You will soon begin to discover that there is a movement, a gait within the lines of his poems and hence within the poem itself.

Some words sound strong and others weak which, with the variation in the length of the line, alters the flow of the sound and makes the poem pleasurable. His rhyming can be as simple as it is intricate. Read the poem *Sister Gone*. The line ending, the rhyming word, of each eight-lined verse is a a, b b, c c c, d. Odd! Not so. Within the last line of each of the three verses you will see a pattern of internal rhyming: 'So high ... against the evening sky'; 'So sad, ... though hitherto so glad'; 'All black ... with light behind her back'.This is the last verse of that poem [Jones: p727].

> *It saddened me that moonpaled night*
> *To see her by the wall, in white,*
> *While friends departed mate with mate*
> *Beyond the often-swinging gate,*
> *As there beside the lilac shade,*
> *Where golden-chained laburnum sway'd,*
> *Around her face her hairlocks play'd*
> *All black with light behind her back*

And as so often happens with Barnes, he quietly describes the person and in doing so describes their circumstance. Despite the Barnes lament found in so many of his poems the last verse of *Sister Gone* is so full of colour, from white to gold, from lilac to black and for Jane, the sister left behind, there is a particular affection, indeed a caress.

Barnes was not a poet full of high drama in the utopian genre – there were little local dramas. Nor one who made a habit of writing poems of vast length on classical subjects – he simply told a tale, usually rural in character, sometimes humorous, sometimes sad, often with a moral and Christian content and usually in this odd Dorset dialect. And he had the annoying habit of when he said what he felt he had to say – when he felt he had told his tale – he simply ended the poem. He seems to disregard the reader who may want to know just a little bit more. A good example is his poem *Whitsuntide an' Club Walken* [Jones: p101]. As a form of collective social service many of the rural poor paid a small weekly contribution into a 'club' and in emergencies, such as sickness and death, the 'club' paid out money to its members to cover their expenses. Each year they met – rather the men met – in the public-house to dispose of the balance of funds in drinking and eating. They put on their best suits, often held a church service, but generally just skylarked and marched about behind their various club banners. 'Young Mary' made a point of getting up early to go and watch the clubmen:

An' down along the road they done
All sorts o' mad-cap things vor fun;
An' danc'd, a-poken out their poles,
An' pushen bwoys down into holes:
An' Sammy Stubbs come out o' rank,
An' kiss'd me up agean the bank,
A saucy chap; I ha'nt vorgi'ed en
Not yet, – in short, I han't a-zeed en.
Zoo in the dusk ov evenen, zome
Went back to drink, an' zome went hwome.

And there the poem ends. Do you see what I mean?

Barnes did not like change. If there was to be change it had to be done slowly. A very worthy Dorset attitude. He enjoyed the simple but practical life, having very few material needs. In this highly technical world perhaps he has given us a pointer; we should stop and look at some of the 'old values' set out in his poems and then maybe do something about them before it is too late.

Glossary

In addition to the Dorset dialect, Barnes wanted to have a simplified 'pure' Anglo-Saxon speech; he did not want Latinised or French words included in the English language. For example, by using the suffix of 'lore' and 'stead' he substituted the names of sciences and places for simple and, what he considered, easily understood words.

ornithology, birdlore
pathology, painlore
geology, earthlore
astronomy, starlore
optics, lightlore
aviary, birdstead
menagerie, animal stead
asylum, safestead
museum, lorestead
laboratory, workstead

There are a few other 'word-endings' in addition to the two given.

At about the same time he also increased his native terms.

resemblance, suchness
clothed, cladness
negative, naysome
universal, allsome
quantity, muchness
explained, outshown
thought, redeship
preface, fore-say.
photograph, sunprint
lunatic, moonmad
terminus, rail-end
remote, outstep
dictionary, word-book

And there are many more but few were ever adopted.

Words from his Glossary

A-feard: afraid

Aggy: corner with sharp joints; a very thin man
 Also to gather eggs

Airmouse: the bat

Aish: the ash tree

Anigh: near to

A-pisty-poll: a mode of carrying a child with his legs on one's shoulders and his arms round one's neck or forehead

Archet: orchard

A-strout: stretched out stiffly like frozen linen

A-stooded: sunk (as waggon wheels) into the ground

Ax: to ask

Bangen: banging. Used as an intensitive as in a 'bangen girt apple.'

Bargen: a small farm or homestead

Barken: a grange yard; a barton

Barm: yeast

Bennets: the stems and flower heads of grass

Bide: to dwell, abide or stay

Bissen: bist (is) not; art not

Blather: a bladder

Blooth: the blossom of fruit trees

Braler: a bundle of straw

Branten: bold; impudent

Bron or Backbran: a large log of wood put on at the back of the fire, particularly at merrymakings in winter

Bundle: to walk hastily

Caddle: confusion; noise

Charm: a noise or confusion of voices, as of children or birds

Childern: children

Chile: child

Clavy: a mantelpiece

Clim': to climb

Clote: the yellow water lily

Cole or Coll: to take one fondly round the neck

Crimp: a little bit

Cubby-hole: a snug place for a child, as between his father's knees

Culver: the wood-pigeon or ring-dove

Daps: to bound as a ball
Didden: did not
Drashel: a flail; also a threshold
Drong or Drongway: a narrow way between two hedges or walls
Drow: to throw
Dumbledore: the humblebee
Ees: yes
Ee-grass: aftermath
Elem: elm
Eltrot: the stalk of the wild parsley
Emmet-but: an ant hill
En: him
Eth: earth
Evemen: evening
Faddle: a pack or bundle
Fay: to succeed; go on favourably
Feace: face
Flip: very kindly or friendly in talking
Footy: little or insignificant
Frith: brushwood
Gawk: to go or stand and stare about idly
Geat: a gate
Gi'e: to give
Gil'cup: the buttercup
Girt: great; big
Greygle: the bluebell
Gwain: going
Hame: the stalks of plants; as beanhame; peashame
Handy: near
Hag-rod: hag-ridden
Hayward: a warden of the common land
Heal: to cover
Heft: weight
He'th: hearth
Het: heat
Hide: to whip
Ho: to be careful or anxious
Hobble: to tie an animal's legs to keep him from wandering
Hodmadod: a mess
Holler: a hollow in a wood; a vale

Housen: a house
Hwomely: friendly
Humstrum: a rude musical instrument
In coose: of course
It: a beating or scolding; 'you'll get it'
Jay: joy
Jiffy: a moment of time
Kaile; cabbage
Kimberlin: not a Portlander; a mainlander.
Knapp: a small hillock or rising
Laggens: short gaiters
Lawk: a word of surprise among females
Lease-carn: corn gleaned
Leaze: a field stocked through the summer
Leery: empty in the stomach
Lewth: shelter from the wind
Lippen: wet; rainy
Litty: of light and easily bodily motion
Love-chile: an illegitimate child
Mampus: a crowd
Me'th: mirth
Mid: may or might
Min: mind; mind you
Mixen: a dung heap
Mussen: must not
Nammet: a luncheon
Nar: never
Nesh: soft; tender
Nicky: very small short-cut bundles of wood for lighting coal fires
Noggerhead: a blockhead
Noo-when: at no time
Nunch: the noon meal
Ooser, or Oose: a mask with opening jaws put on to frighten folk
Orts: waste hay left by cows fed a-field
Pank: to pant
Parrick: a paddock
Peart: well; lively
Pirty: pretty
Pitch: the quantity taken up at once on a hay-fork or pitch-fork
Pleck: a small enclosure

Plim: to swell
Ponted: tainted
Pook: large coned heaps of hay
Puxy: a miry or boggy place
Quaddle: to make limp or flabby
Quiine: a corner of a wall
Randy: a merry-making
Rangle: to wind, like climbing plants
Ratch: to stretch
Rate: to scold
Readship: sense; reason
Reamy: stringy; spoken of slack bread
Reddick: the robin-redbreast
Reremouse: a bat
Rottletraps: rickety old household-goods
Rudge: ridge of roof
Ruf: a roof
Rue: sorrow
Scammish: awkward
Scrag: stunted shrubs
Scroff: small bits of dead wood fallen under trees
Scuoce: to barter
Settle: a long seat with a high plank back
Sheaded: shaded
Sheen: to shine
Shere: shire or county
Skew-whiff: distorted
Skit: to run or walk lightly
Snead: the pole of a scythe
Sog: to saturate or loosen with wet
Somewhen: at some time
Spars: sharp sticks; used by thatchers
Sprack: lively; active
Sumple: supple
Swipes: very thin beer
Swop: to barter
Tallet: a hayloft over a stable
Tantrum: a fit of excitement
Tiaties: potatoes
Tidden: 'tis not

Tillage: digging
Touse: a very slight blow with the hand
Tranter: a common carrier
Traps: goods; tools, and so on
Tun: the chimney-top from the ridge of the house
Tutty: a bunch of flowers or nosegay
Twite: to reproach or mock
Upzides wi': even with
Var: for
Vess: a verse
Viary-ring: a fairy-ring
Vinny: mouldy, or mildewy, from damp
Vlee: to fly
Vlaire: to stream out like hair in the wind
Vo'ke: folk
Vower: four
Vooty: small
Vust: first
Vuz: furze
Wag: to stir
Werden: were not
Werrit: to worry; to teaze
Wevet: a cobweb
Whindlen: small and weakly
Whur: to fling overhanded
Widdock: a small whithe or twig
Woose: worse
Woppen: big; weighty
Wrout: to grub up, as pigs do the ground
Wuth: worth
Ya: you
Yakker: an acorn
Za: to saw
Zennit: seven nights; a week
Zich: such
Zive: scythe
Zoo: so
Zot: sat
Zull: a plough
Zummat: something

Bibliography

To begin to know Barnes it is helpful to read the correspondence, notes, newspaper cuttings etc., contained in his scrapbooks now on microfilm at the Dorset County Museum and the Dorset County Record Office. For the committed researcher, under controlled conditions and approval of the Curator, there are sermons, notebooks, correspondence and some photographs available in the Dorset County Museum.

The Dorset County Library has a delightful collection of books by or about Barnes. And they have more. There are files with newspaper reports and cuttings, the Dorset County Chronicle on micro film, the National Census returns, all sorts of interesting items which add to the enjoyment of the reader and researcher. Their *Dictionary of National Biography* is also important in order to discover details of the lives of many of Barnes's friends.

There are certain musts. Lucy Baxter's biography of her father is essential reading. Giles Dugdale, although producing some new information, does not advance to any great extent and some of his facts are not well researched. But enjoy the outstanding comments and vast quantity of information found in Trevor Hearl's study of Barnes which, although the title apparently limits the book's contents to Barnes as a schoolmaster in fact covers the whole of his life. Then read the gentle book by Alan Chedzoy and you will be well pleased.

Barnes, Col. Lawrance, *The Lineage of Willam Barnes of Dorset*, Swanage, Dorset, 1956.

Barnes, William Miles, *Poems of Rural Life in the Dorset Dialect. Edited by his Son*, Kegan Paul etc., 1909.

Baxter, Lucy Barnes, [Leader Scott], *The Life of William Barnes. Poet and Philologist*, MacMillan, 1887.

Bradbury, Dr Richard and Exeter University, *William Barnes: Collected Prose Works*, Thoemmes Press; Routledge, London, 1996.

Chedzoy, Alan, *William Barnes: A Life of the Dorset Poet*, The Dovecote Press, 1985.

Drinkwater, John, *Twenty poems in Common English by William Barnes*, Basil Blackwell, Oxford, 1925.

Dugdale, Giles, *William Barnes of Dorset*, Cassell & Co., 1953.

Hearl, Trevor W., *William Barnes the Schoolmaster*, Longmans, Dorchester, 1966.

Hardy, Thomas, *Select Poems of William Barnes*, Henry Froude, 1908.

Hinchy, F.S, *The Dorset William Barnes*, F.S and V.M.Hinchy, Blandford, 1966.

Jacobs, Willis D., *William Barnes Linguist*, University of New Mexico Press, 1952.

Jones, Bernard, *The Poems of William Barnes*, in two volumes, Centaur Press, London, 1962

Laurence Keen and Charlotte Lindgren, *William Barnes, The Dorset Engravings*, DNHAS, Dorchester, 1986.

Levy, William Turner, *The Man and his Poems*, Longmans, Dorchester, 1960.

Motion, Andrew, *William Barnes Selected Poems*, Penguin Books, 1994.

Oliver, Vere L., *Late William Barnes as an Engraver*, Friary Press, Dorchester, 1925.

Parins, James W., *William Barnes*, Twayne Publishers, Boston, 1984.

Wrigley, Christopher, *William Barnes, The Dorset Poet*, The Dovecote Press, 1984.

Recordings

Lydlinch Bells, Dialect Poetry of William Barnes, Forest Tracks, Poole, 1978.

Blackmore by the Stour, Dorset Dialect Poems by William Barnes, by Tim Laycock, Forest Tracks, Poole, 1985.

Index

Douglas Ashdown was the founder member of the William Barnes Society (1983). He was educated at Poole Grammar School, served in the Royal Navy during the Second World War, qualified as a Chartered Public Accountant and worked in local government as a senior officer in treasurer's departments for some forty years, mainly with Dorset County Council. He is committed to bringing the pleasures of knowing Barnes's work to a wider audience and to that end has researched Barnes and his family for the past ten years. He lectures to local groups and is a member of the Society of Dorset Men.

This introduction is a layman's view of William Barnes and is an attempt to stimulate ordinary folk, particularly of Dorset, into realizing the humour, the gentleness and the common sense which this man showed towards his fellow man. Much of what he wrote and did is as relevant today as it was then. His wide range of practical and academic accomplishments is lightly touched upon in this essay and the hope is that other facets of this extraordinary scholar will be researched.

Very little has been published about Barnes during the last ten years despite the activity of the Society and newly discovered material. This trend should be reversed, particularly as the year 2001 will mark the bicentenary of his birth.

The stated aims of the William Barnes Society are 'to enable members to share fellowship and pleasure in the life and work of William Barnes. Its membership includes scholars and laymen, those chiefly interested in his poetry and others who are drawn by his connection with Dorset history and dialect'. To this end lectures, readings, summer schools and expeditions are organised. In February of each year a Service of Remembrance for the life and work of William Barnes is held at Winterborne Came Church, near Dorchester.